The Sound We Make Ourselves

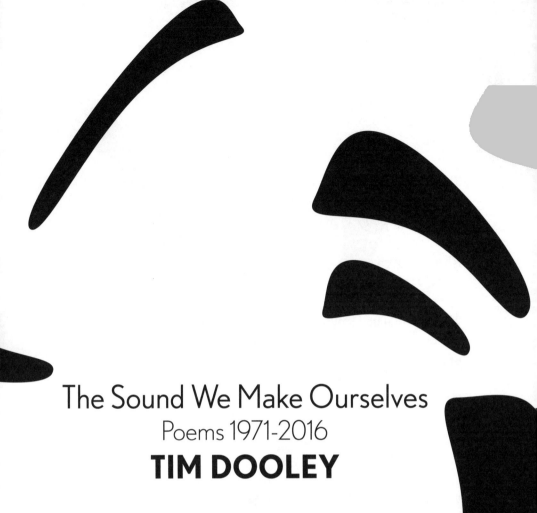

The Sound We Make Ourselves
Poems 1971-2016
TIM DOOLEY

 **EYEWEAR** PUBLISHING

First published in 2016
by Eyewear Publishing Ltd
Suite 333, 19-21 Crawford Street
Marylebone, London W1H 1PJ
United Kingdom

Typeset with graphic design by Edwin Smet
Author photograph by Bev Robinson
Printed in England by TJ International Ltd, Padstow, Cornwall

The right of Tim Dooley to be identified as author of
this work has been asserted in accordance with section 77
of the Copyright, Designs and Patents Act 1988
ISBN 978-1-911335-50-4

Eyewear wishes to thank Jonathan Wonham
for his generous patronage of our press.

WWW.EYEWEARPUBLISHING.COM

for my students
past and present

TABLE OF CONTENTS

PART ONE: 1971-1987

PART TWO: 1988-1997

PART THREE: 1998-2016

TIM DOOLEY
is a tutor for The Poetry School
and a visiting lecturer at the University of Westminster.
He was a teacher for many years – a head of department in
two comprehensive schools and a senior tutor in a tertiary
college. He has also taught poetry at Goldsmiths College
and been an arts mentor for the Koestler Trust, as well as
reviewing for the *TLS* and writing obituaries for the
Times. He has been reviews and features editor of
Poetry London since 2008 and will complete his
term in that role in Spring 2017.

His first collection of poems, *The Interrupted Dream,*
was published by Anvil in 1985. This was followed by the
pamphlets *The Secret Ministry* (2001) and *Tenderness* (2004),
both winners in the Smith/Doorstop-Poetry Business
pamphlet competition. *Tenderness* was also a Poetry Book
Society Pamphlet Choice. *Keeping Time* (Salt, 2008)
was a Poetry Book Society Recommendation.
It was followed by *Imagined Rooms* (Salt, 2010).

PART ONE
1971-1987

Let our poetry be… impure as the clothing we wear,
or our bodies stained with soup or shame – our wrinkles,
night-wakings, dreams; declarations of loathing and love;
loyalties, denials and doubts; affirmations of faith
and payments of taxes.

– after Pablo Neruda

HOMEFINDING

If you find the new place, and when you've climbed
the stairs, unpacked each case and closed with care
each unfamiliar door, perhaps you'll stare
through these clean windows or, later, leaning
on the desk, you'll turn your head and say, 'I'm
glad we chose this place and glad I'm leaving

where I was before. The walls look older
here. Back then I hated walls. I thought they
kept all life outside and it was colder
when they curled around me. I kept away
from rooms before, but now so much has changed.
I like that chair; those flowers you've arranged.'

The new place is like that. It stuns us by
its size. We didn't think that warmth would flow
through pipes like that and make no sound. The high
ceilings are light, unstained and even. No
breeze disturbs a curtain, even less
your tired face, your rest. I'm sure you'll find
the place quite soon and hope that you won't mind
when you arrive, my asking the address.

ALFOXDEN 1798 (PROBLEMS IN CRITICISM)

                      'Query: Are
the male and female flowers on separate trees?'
'The day cold'
           – and, returning from her visit
to Holford Woods, Wordsworth's sister
                   (called exquisite
by his discerning friend, the noted critic)
      wrote these
             words inside her journal.

     'On separate trees.'
What could she mean describing hollies so? Is it
a symbol born from melancholic whim
         that she's
just left for Will to pick at?
I'll accept with ease
Whatever explanation experts posit.

     …rather that than wonder why words freeze
each time we touch
          or ask 'What is it?'
leaves us
      wooden,
          forked
             apart.

ITINERANTS

In this wrecked country
where dry-stone walls
once half-built, now
half-fallen, protect
nothing badly – you
wonder how it is
the people live. Wind
tears at leaf-stripped
trees and rain bares
rock of a soil that's
scarcely natural.

The van rattles,
rasping with Irish
on this fourth day
of storm. Packs on
separate shoulders,
we neither touch
nor quarrel. I watch
your tongue tracing
the margin of your
mouth as if a smile,
or something, were
suddenly to begin.

LEVEL CROSSING

Who are the crazed ecologists
conserving dust in corners of our room?

Pity is in association for the microbe.
Appetite is browning like a steak.

We home to ancient manners; cigarettes
are finger-rolled. Billiard balls collide,

on contact crash down mushrooms, slide
into a hole. Beer's hopped, hand-pumped

and downed where old men's cheeks
are local colour, fields are sown.

Tractors with searchlights tear at earth.
Wild geese and waders know the times of trains.

The cars will queue at the level crossing.
The railwayman will drag the gates.

In five years' time you stand him drinks
and hear of his arthritic hip.

HANWORTH

Off the new motorway, downstairs,
a thirties suburb sleeps. In grey
light, people shop or move pushchairs
along. We feel the bone-cold day
around us and walk fast through streets
that brand-names decorate. The paid-for
signs reflect where cloudwork meets
with brick, interrupt affairs
of blankness where couples stroll
by glass-front shops, assess and price
the packaged goods.
                              As if the whole
story were theirs, or this cool place
something they had warmed to – they walk
as careful lovers, light, in pace
with the placid day. Soft as talk
at distance, hidden like a soul,
the outer borough nurtures life,
continues, weathering like chalk
to turns of time.
                              Husband or wife,
at one remove from rumour, smiles.
Between these flowerbeds there's still
a sense of sharing. The road trails
off. In a few streets' time, fields will
show horses beyond a child's belief.
Green intervals protected still from grief.

ALISON

In the wide-framed window she is wiping,
I see a view like guide-book pictures:
the place, its abbey and antiquities.
This is not the day to view it. She shivers
as the rain falls steadily outside.

She is settling into marriage as the
winter settles into Bath. His clever
talk is not what she remembers. There
are noises where he hit her on the ear.

Free talk. Free love. Among the interference
she senses memories of sex, athletic,
like a comic muzak. Buzzes echo
a passionate frankness that went off key.

She is settling to marriage, accepting
with strange humour. She has wiped the glass
with patience. She wants to make it clean.

PERSON: TENSE AND NUMBER

Arrive in November and on the latest train
to walk through the brewery smells cutting
the river to the dead city centre. Then climb
a mile's light silence plus your shoes' echo
by Victorian growth up to newer suburbs. I've
other ways of approaching – 'have had' – that
imitate a safe return, so that reaching the top
of the town is smoothly relaxing a grip.

'Was'. With the early returns appropriated
and no investment forthcoming, it is lack now
dominates. Street corners exhale contextless
ghosts with guilt edging, that shiver and
embarrass. This place is consigned for memory.
Presence is of mind to sink in the capital among
the married mass, at professional parties
forgetting foundations. Formal. A face

that concerns itself with erasure, accretion
(so as to not lose face). It is taking a rhythm
from the underground: distortions of doubled
glass muddy it. It seeps into oligocene loam.
Weekends are escapes. The deep country dark
is desirable, playing the soundtrack from a
retreat. Reflection can be avoided. A mirror
and white walls is not what I asked for.

32ºC

The Trident is doing its diagonal overhead drone
while an amazement of starlings makes scattering
manoeuvres about twilight. We sit on the stone steps.
It is high June and full heat that shocks newspapers
persists in still air. We are in gratitude for the day
and its prospect that seems to open on a street whose
trees are comfortable like wealth. Only at this close
a fluttering comes of faith, an itch, almost a gasp.

We are watching from a house out of the nineteenth
century, looking down from its steps on a garden we've
no strong wish to tend. The street we desire is in
shadow from this other street. The indifferent suburb,
where you sense indifference in a dull wash like
variations in car design or fashions of urban renewal,
is part of our unease and as large as bowel movements
or dry throbbing light in our reading of the day.

What feels like a gasp out of the nineteenth century,
a *let us be true to one another* flung in unbelief
at sea, signifies hope that small trusting creatures
can learn to share living. We touch to that rhythm
and glance indoors at the ephemera of love, collected.
We know something that the street has learned, if we
cannot know the street. While starlings return to
their wire, the Trident ends its long escaping roar.

NOS MEILLEURS CLICHÉS

The queues in the motorway cafés are moving
more slowly this summer; but there's a lot of
lively talk on the road to egg, sausage and beans.
An excitement has started as we head south,
dressed for the parallel life. This pause is the
arena of our anxious planning. We compute
forgotten supplies, check times of arrival
to tunes of pre-cooked food and corporate décor.

The papers are keeping us awake with cricket
victories or the death of Presley. They help our
digestion, until we are already glowing with
greedy thoughts of what we might bring back.
Me by Hotel X. Loved ones near the Prado.
Mountains and beaches are waiting in sunlight
for recording eyes and we will snap them up as
bargain backdrops for our self-display. We have

the scenes already framed and squared and
we are in them. Now the image we'll treasure
(what never quite happened) is prepared in the
heart. Something to meditate on in winter years,
against troubled children or lack of money. When
the best evenings are brought down to the language
of Rupert Murdoch. 'Look', you will say,
'the year of cricket and the death of Chaplin'.

THE STRANGE CONVERSIONS

He opens the door: black shirt, black jeans. The day,
he says, has an affinity with black. The neutron bomb
is in his speech while a woman is reading fresh accounts
of rape. Knife wounds erupt in any smirk until a bolt and
chain is snapped across each opening of light. Their right
to fear closes the syllogism. A darkness in the rain
no conspiracy explains. Smashed lights at the pedestrian
crossing, supermarket trolleys abandoned like streets.

A corner in any Western city. Communist posters
slapped on the face of Sir 'Jimmy' Goldsmith, alternative
theatre in an unlikely pub. And on the end of a terrace
or unused wall the bright realist mural appears. Simplified
workers defy abstract bulldozers beneath cartoon cranes.
Near Pernety or Kentish Town the half-planned decades
collide in carnival. Optimists of agitprop rehearse in the
co-operative restaurant, waiting for their notice to quit.

The year is closing in and news of friends arrives.
The schoolboy radical joins the Ministry of Defence.
The born-again Christian contemplates adultery.
How they disappoint, these parodies of betrayal.
Like the smell of something rotting, this lethargy
that fudges every act. Convictions cancelling
each other out until I cannot imagine change.
Only an empty planet, a passive mind erased.

THE OLD WORSHIP

On Station Road the rockabilly fans cradling loud
cassette players slouch with brutal authority like
connoisseurs of art. You arrive with a standard –
lamp and flowers in your hat. My druid priestess.
It is Saturday in the tiresome world – too late to
start a religion. We make our way along a pavement
crowded with difficulty: unsure who is still
friendly to us, whom we should pretend to love.

There is the library to be comfortable in when
your thoughts chatter. Hear the microprint index
whirr. It flies through an orchard of shelves,
their branches heavy with cling-film coloured fruit.
Maybe today there will be something new. My
shining notes glitter in their ache for synthesis.
Beyond the modern glass, the car park with its
new thin trees waits respectfully for spring.

Or perhaps there is sorting our furniture again,
moving the carpet we are not tired of, getting
a fresh hold on the room. Then we will be ready
for the cosy months, the long days we take refuge
in. There will be time for sacred music and time for
distractions. Hope for that. Let us ignore the
brown packet of letters, the unfamiliar hand,
the old thin words of those we have failed to love.

'HIS BEST PIECE OF POETRIE'

His face in the cot is his great-grandmother's face.
The face his mother places in a frame downstairs
retains his anxious smile. In that brown-mottled
photograph, a woman sits on the awkward edge
of a bentwood chair. She wears a Regency striped dress
the son who barely knew her remembers as blue. Her fur-trimmed
coat will not take off the chill of fear, as she looks out to us –
who taste the times she did not live to understand.

Tigris and Suir, Tawe and the Manchester Ship Canal.
Will he see the waters where his elders wept?
Innocent of thought, Sam gurgles in his sleep, a blue
tortoise rising on his slowcoach moving chest.
Armenians in Baghdad before a genocidal war; Irish
impatient for their dignity. Those who fled their patriarchs
or misers for a small secure success, for England's late
complacency – migrate to his quiet breath and heart.

When he comes of age in quite another century,
what will he think of them among what other sorrows?
From the dark future he'll look back at someone
else's dream. A dream of all the centuries – and we
who wish him only joy may not be wise enough to grasp
its meaning. I feel the grip of the dear hand that circles
my small finger. As strong as hope. And think about
Ben Jonson's words, his child who died at seven.

A PART OF THE MAIN

A figure in a one-man boat
is pulling from his seine
fish that are strange to us.

On handkerchiefs of land
grow plantains, peppers, fruit.

He steers between these fields
watching water shake itself
like a tall haze of sky.

The shining evening spins ahead:
his empty market tray,

or ice in a long glass of rum.
The tapir-driven taxis pass.
Men talk of bat and ball.

I am reading essays
for the overseas exam.

Through the poorly-puttied window
close wooden fences lean
like the walls of a shanty town.

The script lies open
on a small metal desk.

Mr. Persaud writing.
He wants to take a post
in some other, foreign country.

Poor prospects, rigidity,
botched new developments.

He hopes for wealth, smart buildings
and: 'if I walk by a lake
with a girlfriend, no-one would talk.'

In my lakeless suburb
this back view of a house:

A figure in a lighted room
is reading on lined paper
words that are strange to him.

An Edward Hopper figure
in the static placeless night.

A clothed figure held up by light,
in the night where the world turns
and home is abolished.

Wondering what it would be like
in another, foreign country.

The zig-zag fire escapes,
fresh coffee, pretzels,
the rattling Legendary El.

Someone else's map invades
the starless blank through which we move.

We wear imported clothes,
eat fresh exotic fruit.
This news I hear – the Cortes

at gunpoint on all fours –
is local and is real.

Griefs pin-prick the night to form
reflecting the reclaimed land
we steer through with our days,

joined by some work or hope,
a message from another country

something glimpsed rocking
in the prow of a fisherman's boat,
wrapped in a coloured magazine.

We had to bring it along
so nothing would be strange to us.

A FORBIDDING SPRING

There's nothing charming
about rain on a March Saturday, or a family breakfast
    with attention divided
between window and room – forgetting one's words
    to focus for a moment
on daffodils that look in at us, soaking and hurt,
    or a single item of news.

I'm beginning to panic
about messages that remain unheard, legal silencings.
    Notes pass from hand to hand
to be lost unaccountably; letters are damaged in transit.
    Or those who pass words on
are damaged unaccountably; their movements limited.
    The whistleblower's jailed.

The tunnels are policed.
'When the cat goes off, the rhythm of steel on concrete.
    Against the fact of torture,
we imagine a truth in the other prisoners' lies.'
    When word of such words
leaks out, it is the occasion of arrest and exile.
    We've yet to know the worst.

Today it is only rain.
They don't tell us what was said at night, how
    the classified cables
have tied our tongues, twisting the torque
    of what's not said in love.
'I can't tell a joke with the new forms of speech
    still less write a poem.'

Can his poem outlive
the leader he'd attack? The innocent in office
        posts an incriminating file.
Our friends are preparing for the great march
        to the old town square.
Will we join them this year? Or is it time
        to send the polite reply
that blames an awkward age, or the forbidding weather?

WOMAN READING

Matisse, *La Liseuse*

Dark green chenille, I think, hangs
half over the cupboard drawer
and your few 'precious things'
– that piece of jade, a lamp,
nothing contemporary –
weigh down the corner in a crowd of detail.
I see you from behind,
leaf-filtered light striking a neck
white as the book's slim vee.
It feeds you – perching on one hand,
perplexing, silent bird –
like memory, or deep orange ochre
in the postcard that marks a page.

In that early study, you confront
torched mines and noisy factories…
troubles wide and dark…an easy wheel
that sets sharp racks at work,
cold college rooms, persistent literature
that sets the heart's intents
to thought and struggle: banners red
as Keats's warm expectorated blood.

The later work
has you across from me;
an angled arm supports
your sleepy head and papers lie
along a table tangent to your chair.
A pierglass takes the light
and throws your tessellated profile out,
scarlet and black, knee over thigh,
in modern dress. A dream continuing
beneath flowers, framed photographs.

A terrible childbed hast thou had,
my dear. At rest, this evening,
you turn to Pericles' persistence,
to scenes where women's words
changed stubborn destinies.

Against a background of black,
your mind still turns on words,
still hoping to uncover
some complex source of light.

CONTRE-JOUR *(portraits of Ezra Pound)*

that mastery of ink and brush
             the chisel's grave hierarchy
                       accepted
but Avedon's photograph
             6.30.58
                       Rutherford New Jersey
cut citrus sun-dried
             a thin shirt draped
                       on the coarse cloth skin
they saved for him
             sore lips threatening speech
                       the Titan's loose robe
without Kent or Cordelia
             the eyelid's sewn purse
                       holding something back
or shut against too much light

'BALLOONS'

Kennedy's promise
to 'put a man on
the moon – and bring
him back' or is it
the harmonica break
in 'Love me Do'?

Anything with 1963
written under it
rather than a February
room in Primrose Hill
with snow six weeks old
still crackling and stiff.

She moves between two
children and a typewriter,
noticing those oval,
brightly coloured moons
of air; stepping closer to
the crackling lunar edge.

THE SOUTH

The popular songs
of our language stress the
difference of this borderline.
Below the Rio Grande on
the peripheral freeway of
the world's largest city, she
changes down dawdling
behind the shaky *camión*
longer than she'd thought it
would take to notice
the fragile covering of skin,
the dead shanks rattling
outside the tarpaulin.
In Africa she'd left her
camera in the hotel, offering
no offence to the remnant
of a shirt, six pieces of fruit
or single row of nuts
arranged for market day.
In postmodern Middlesex,
vernacular brick and
glass stained brown watch
a wind disturb the stray
image of limbs trapped
by fallen plaster, the paper-
thin coverage of the shy
Nyala. A man in ageing
tweeds offers three suits
on a rail. A jukebox leaks
Mi amor, mi corazón.

CUSTOMS OF THE PROVINCE

The legends concerning
how we appear on the surface
of a lake or a much slid-on stone
are a requirement of faith.

In the pale early years,
a white costume was called for.
Now we mostly sleep and eat.

A forklift-truckful of bamboo
passes through the best of us
between darknesses.

In memory of the girl
whose skin was peach-blossom
we dip our hands and feet in pitch.

In memory of the tiger's anger
and our sad survival here,
we wipe our eyes with stained hands.

So you stare at us
and we return your gaze,
looking out sparingly
from behind twin moons of kohl.

THE UNBURDENING ROOM

A wooden
structure about
the size of a
gardening shed
in which a
window is fixed
open for native
wildflowers, a
yawning chasm,
but as well
the voices you
crossed a city not
expecting to hear.
Beside the stream
leaves leak like
eggs through
brown paper.
The rocks the
river runs
through are walls
of a disused mill.

She heard
something in the
music driving
back to England
a week ago like
voices out of
childhood. The
Sunday Latin he
reeled away
from, grey stone
against an
unrelieved grey
sky. When rain
relents, light
touches a patch
of skin or grasses
shift with the
prevailing wind,
an accidental
nimbus rewards
the patient stare.

CONDUIT

A stone's throw
from Fleet
Ditch the
plastic cup of
wine taken
from me and a
face I start to
recompose.
We are Nabis
of the text. Mr
4 am's dark
glasses share a
flat December
surface with
poems of failed
marriage, a
balcony open to
night's cries,
flecks in the
retina, urine
examined for
portents.
It has been
taken from me,
the beautiful
skin tones of
the young, gull-
shrieks off the
Atlantic,
a child lost in
walkways of
dapple grey.

THE SOUND WE MAKE OURSELVES

A tamed assault-
course. This latest in play furniture; climbing frames
            of slatted pine,
tyre steps, a ladder bridge and – almost
            at arm's length
and harmless below the enflamed trees –
            the sun's quiet fire
returning some coolness in our stare.

A week ago,
on Broadwater Farm – as, once, in Divis Flats
            front doors collapsed
at dawn to our concern. Like uniformed men,
            stepping over
a woman who may or may not be dying,
            we are vague
about detail and take slowly to speech.

We're catching up
on other news, old friendship calling back
            a flickering warmth.
In the hall of the home you're outgrowing:
            a daughter's picture,
the rings of paint she added to your work
            and jagged drawings
done with the left hand, against habits of style.

                    Yesterday,
        light like this caught a three-foot profile
                    on the green canal
        as my son stopped to listen on our walk and said
                    he heard two things:
        the bird's expected music in the trees and,
                    what I'd not heard,
        our shoesteps crashing through the new crisp leaves.

PART TWO
1988-1997

The young are quick of speech.
Grown middle-aged, I teach
Corrosion and distrust,
Exacting what I must.

– from *Yvor Winters*
'On Teaching the Young'.

NIGHT SHIFT

Phillipe Jaccottet, *Le Travail du Poète*

We're like night-watchmen,
our eyes more salmon-red
at each hour's end, but not
from crying or a dream's
disturbance – we're pastors
naming every item left at risk,
all to be lost should sleep
disturb our husbandry.

CLASS

Alvin's red Pringle
is well the business
and Shital's Kappa top
rumoured to be crucial.

Carrie was telling Keri
all about Mu Lin's double
reverse tuck into seatdrop
when the bell went.

I blew the whistle. Now
I watch the last, the least
keen forms shuffle
into the building,

before the gulls'
shrieking sharp descent,
white-grey against grey-black
from corners of the roof,

investigating crisp packets —
one frantic group tearing
apart an unfinished roll.
Soon I'll be hurrying back

where this serious shared
business goes happily,
noisily on: maiming,
remodelling our words.

AFTER NERUDA

Pablo Neruda, *Walking Around*

Sometimes he's tired of being a man.
The reflection he sees, in shopwindows
or the cinema screen, takes on a sad
substance, tired and withered: ash-stains
on a shiny piece of suit cloth.

The gents hairdressers, with its cocktail
of smells, stings him to tears.
He wants the sleep of wool or old stones,
to see nothing of enterprises or gardens,
nothing of merchandise, spectacles, lifts.

He's tired of his feet, of toe-clippings,
of hair everywhere. Of his shadow.
He's just tired of being a man,
waking like a root in a dark cellar,
absorbing, thinking, counting the dead.

And Monday is the screech of a tyre,
or a sudden petrol flare.
It sees him coming with his prison face,
sends him to hospitals where bones fall out of
the windows, to damp and vinegary stores.

So he walks around, for peace, for forgetfulness,
past caged birds the colour of sulphur, tripe,
dentures in a coffee pot, surgical appliances,
and old men's underclothes hanging from a line,
weeping their slow, dirty tears.

THE MILKY WAY

The marble features of the Parthenon frieze
                    aren't the only things
to seem flatter and greyer since the summer
                    you were sixteen.

O'Driscoll remembers the white bicycles
                    those other Provos
left on Amsterdam street corners for free
                    and common use.

There were pictures from museums on the train
                    and songs of that time
in the background, the five days we crossed
                    from the Stedelijk

to Jordaan's brown cafés. It was later though,
                    with wanted posters
for the Red Army Fraction pasted on a wall
                    at the terminus.

There were screams in the night, soft cheese
                    and jam at breakfast.
A tape of Bukka White barely troubled the
                    glittering meniscus

of your genever, or the couple chopping a black
                    cube into silver-
paper deals: their downy daughter snoozing
                    on the bar.

We shared a four bunk room with transients
                    waiting to buy a car.
Stavros and his cousin were ready to go home
                    — after a decade

in New York, struggling with electronics and
                    English, repairing
beat-up radios, lecturing on Ritsos — to go home
                    to the free use

of their tongue. O'Driscoll is easing his way
                    into the story
of his second time in Holland — peace week
                    at the Melkweg.

Did his disarmament play leave the audience stunned
                    or were they stoned,
like the actors, staring at significant intervals
                    between words?

He wants to tell us about the boat-trip back to Hull,
                    how they disposed
of the stuff — fear and the North Sea at night.
                    I am looking

in your eyes at a different year and the dark
                    sea off Naxos,
a high glittering sky and its reflection,
                    like a window

opening in our marriage, the evening's gifts
                    scattered freely,
like the broad and unmourned highway
                    of spilt milk.

JUNE

The first weeks of Wimbledon
       and the word 'love'
has passed between us like
       zero, or some chosen
absolute. That ochre picture
       – sunpainted Italy –
a trail snapped from a mountain
       in your teens, now
stained by late development
       is in my eye again.

Those first times away from him
       look empty and unfinished,
as we sort your father's things
       and the word 'alone'
opens like a blister in the earth.

PREPARING TO MEET THE DAY

A routine and a rite –
this soaping, scraping away
of the night's crop of maleness.

Rinsing the blade,
as if concealing the evidence –
he catches, in the air,
rank nicotine and silence.

His hand on her shoulder
is no help at all.

A relic from that time
they looked together at the light
we move through,
and towards.

DÉTENTE

A fingertip at play
inside you and my head
cushioned on your breast,
listening like a safe breaker
for some loosening
of the latch.

The thin ice has melted
and the gate's unlocked on
the bridge to the lake's small island,
where rock plants flower – saxifrage
or snowdrops waving tiny
flags of truce.

RESISTANCE

Days after the storm, this unsought fog
holds fireworks' aftersmoke, while streetlights blink
a wasteful orange, forgetful of clocks.

Yellow and pale and brown, our hectic walk
to school fills with fragmented leaves,
faces passing, familiar multitudes.

And Shelley was wrong too about the way
the dying leaves hold to the damaged branch
against the force of theory or wind.

Leaves cling like all of us, to purposes
imagined once – the wound forgotten spring
still uncoiling in our steps.

MRS. WU

In '57, he went to see the new Russian.
The great helmsman said, *Rap the guy's knuckles.*
That's no way to behave when Joe ain't hardly dead.
Destalinize… Destabilize!
And Enlai said to Kruschev,
You've taken too much land.

The fat peasant called him bourgeois.
Zhou was still smiling.
Who says we've nothing in common?
We've each betrayed our class.
And he told the story and heard it told again
in Warsaw, Budapest, Belgrade…

Two years before in Bandung:
We must not forget, as Asians,
the first atom bomb fell on our continent…

You know those stories. Long before,
my husband called him blood brother
and paid for his study in Kyoto.

He knew too little Japanese
and, with nothing to spend, took
the woman's part,
clearing the futon and sweeping the room.

In the evenings, we ate what he cooked.
He clung to the wine bottle and argued with Wu.
A strong leader is worthless, unless the people learn.
'And what is strong drink worth?', I asked.
Zhou looked for a broom and next day brought me flowers.

There was blossom for nine days in Maruyama park.
Now nowhere in Kyoto is that bittersweet scent.
Many died. Too many with his name on.
And he too died early, before Zedong,
the word *poems* ambiguous on his lips.

TACT

Unannounced, you sidled
rather than stumbled
into this dream of a blazing
family row. Sitting it out
modestly, looking not unembarrassed
at my performance, moving
your clenched broad fingers
between one another, flexing them
in a gesture between exasperation
and prayer.
        My hectoring voice
wavers as you look abashed at me,
like that skateboarder halting suddenly,
as the hearse climbed the hill to your last
view of the lighthouse and the pier.

You didn't speak, but sat,
an unobtrusive visitor.
Your wild white hair, your moustache
like crests of foam, looking
– not neatly combed and stiff
as we saw them in the chapel of rest –
but as I saw you last alive,
guiding my fledgling driver's eye
to the parking space by the hospital doors.

Or more than twenty years before,
after the last great flare of adolescence,
waking early and without rancour
to drive me to the station and my friends.

Or earlier still, on the day of my sister's birth,
calming us into the car, with words
of the love sons owe to mothers and warnings
against taking sides.

              Which quieten
my raised voice now, accustom me
to the long and patient view
over a perturbed and placid-seeming bay
where, without you, I must learn
your watchful, unassertive gift.

1948 (ELEPHANT AND CASTLE)

Loosening
my tie, in sudden autumn heat,
I look again
at this photograph from forty
years ago
I found on a postcard rack
last Saturday.

Soft-slippered feet resting
on the sill,
as a woman turns her cheek
against his
check-shirt shoulder, waiting
for some kind
word from him, smoking silent
beside her.

Thick white china, a rationed
hunk of fat,
fill the small utility table.
As she looks
in his eyes and he past hers,
the young hurt
faces hold something fragile,
like pre-war
building between them again.

For a moment,
I hear the spray on Margate pier,
     tight young steps
turning to walk back the length of it:
     faces smiling
as if to brave the years' slow
     count of loss,
their long garnering of storm.

SEEING SHELLEY PLAIN

The tall figure with feathering
white hair, crossing the foyer
of the Queen Elizabeth Hall
as if on castors, one arm aloft
holding the largest glass of vodka
in the world, as if this were
the Statue of Liberty's lamp
(and he Paul Revere)
was Robert Lowell.

And when the Poetry Society flunky
added to his censure of flashes
that smoking was not permitted,
Auden's dried apricot face snarled
that he liked cigarettes,
but cameras interfered with his reading.
And what a reading. Parts of the Eddas.
'In Praise of Limestone'. Favourites back to the Thirties.

You could get Bunting then.
Briggflatts almost too often,
but *Chomei at Toyama* unforgettably
and 'a piece WB Yeats did me the honour
of learning by heart'.
Somehow, in the downstairs bar,
we got to talking about how Homer
would have fared on the wireless.

I never saw Stevie Smith (though
my brother did) and I later met people
who'd met David Jones. At college
I vaguely knew a man called Trueblood
who in Venice, on his way from Santa Barbara,
saw almost the last of Ezra Pound,
silent between two aged women.

SEPTEMBER

He's begun reading biographies
and noticing how the cramped
early pages, the three
contrasting accounts
of how the lovers met

give way to vaguenesses,
gaps filled with speculation,
years when the subject might
have visited Tuscany
or acted in an undistinguished role

of which records later vanished.
So, after Sunday lunch,
it seems natural to walk
through the park unnoticed,
or watch others wander past

without acknowledgement,
kicking a crab apple perhaps,
or prising a conker open,
exposing its shiny
coffin-shaded fruit.

NIGHTFALL

Throughout autumn, all through the graduated,
creeping grey of journeys past the railway bridge,
   Lucille noted days on which
   light kept its promises – great
     blocks of pale or darker blue
offset by russets, lemons or maroons.
Businesses thrived or closed. Beggars sang tunes
or sold cheap lighters. She watched the sky for change
until it seemed she reached the end of change.

Darkening days lit up with festivals,
fireworks for Diwali or Guy Fawkes.
   Week-ends meant shorter, damper walks,
   or trips to newly opened malls
     outside the city limits.
This week new Beaujolais. All the next,
displays of party dresses. Under lights,
in air-warmed atria, she felt as if on stage,
as if what haunted her was just a stage

to pass through like the others. Winter colds
hung on longer than before. Foggy air
   left stains on the windscreen of her car.
   All of it made her feel old
     suddenly. Outside, an
ear-ringed, peak-capped boy played 'Nowhere Man',
his dog wrapped in a neat plaid blanket. And
'Happy Christmas (War is Over)' played again
in the lift to the parking floors. And again

small nations' griefs plumped up the weekend press.
Each widow's grief was different and the same.
    Each mother's horror measured as
    a fractured smile, a face undressed.
      Lucille put on her mask,
set out to face the early evening's tasks,
thought again how much the year had asked
of her. At the street's end stood the sky:
the overbearing, weighty, hardened sky.

The dashboard LCD read 16:12.
Tall orange streetlights started to come on.
    Behind them, sulphurous yellow ran
      its course beneath the groaning shelf
        of cloud that thickened still.
Is this how dark it gets? The question Lucille
asked could penetrate the crystalline array
of solid surfaces, enter a space
an angstrom wide, or reach to distant space,

interrogating emptiness of galaxies,
asking non-decreasing event horizons
    what light comes in or out. Reasons,
    arguments – the stuff exegesis
      explores – implode near
a black hole's neither light nor darkened door;
and interstellar spaces no longer hoard
a crown of candles, or some freakish star.
Lucille looked at the clouded night which no star

burst through. Inside houses, coloured balls
cheered wrecked conifers, families found meaning
    in games or company. Nothing
    egregious disturbed decked halls.
        Lucille dropped out of sight.
Without her, little changed. The sky grew lighter
a little longer as the year turned. White
petals broke the soil's crust – the grave of all
kept its secrets... almost like nothing at all.

BRIEF ENCOUNTER

Bonking in Rome,
Goethe tapped hexameters on his mistress's back.
O'Driscoll thought of home,
listening out for the tickety-clack
of rail and wheel that wasn't to be heard
in the air-conditioned carriage.

His fingers worked a brief massage
through the shaggy beard that just
resisted grey. Then a quick
double slap to the cheeks, to wake
himself – or get the touch at least
of something real.

He turned his gaze away from the rail
to the imaginary face
of Eva, his companion. She traced
a letter in the moistened vapour
you don't get in trains these days. *J'ai peur,*
she would have said, had she been French.

But she was American. And language
loped away from her in long arching swirls,
even and intelligent,
naming what went past, examining what was meant
by the latest curl and turn
in what was surely not the march of events.

O'Driscoll considered a sandwich,
observed a chalk horse stretched out against
ancient greenery, and thought
of generations who crept down from hill-forts
to scrape the grass away – their unfenced
world – and what he still called the mind of Man.

The flare of Eva's lucent mind
guttered momently; and he was rising, breathless,
to the story of that Dorset giant, taller
than some cathedrals, with its enormous... *No, a phallus,*
she intercepted briefly
a penis is a great deal smaller.

And he had made her up to cut him down.
Fantastic irony. The train stayed on the track.
all he could do was read his paperback,
sharing romantic sorrows with Young Werther.

ANOTHER PART OF THE CITY

It was dark. He was wet and half a mile west
of where he was meant to be. So he dried out,
nursing a pint of mottled, off-brown best
in the back lounge of a bar that had been named
for some Crimean battle. The street had been lined
with recent cars and fairly healthy trees.

Inside was the usual plush, brasses and polished
wood – and the usual talk he supposed: office
politics, purchases, a hint about creosote, the match;
and an odd running joke about a man called Pritchard.
Pritchard was nothing to him. He would never get the hang
of his story, never know why Godalming was funny or important.

He had tried Pork Scratchings, tried an interest in cricket.
Now he sat with his back to the wall and a pencil
for the crossword. It was beginning to trickle through –
what Eva had told him at the party in Dulwich.
What it means for your face not to fit. To be moon-featured
or differently complexioned, with the magazines gorgeously gaunt.

Or what Gregor had said about his first trip back
in the early days of the thaw. Exhausting welcomes
and a bloke who could tell from his face the exact suburb
his father and uncle had fled from. Not particularly clever.
You needn't know anything about visas or fear – just where the Jews
were likely to have lived. He was getting the message.

It was dark. He was dry, but half a mile west
of where he was meant to be. So he drained down
the remains of his mottled, off-brown best
and left his paper, clueless, on the sagging chair.
It was just that he was off course. Not the weather,
not the map. Pritchard, Godalming. And unfamiliar trees.

PORNOGRAPHY

The day was ending. Darkening air
     would soon take home from labour each
     animal that walks the earth. On this field too
feet stamped. Misty skeins of breath
     rose from glistening lips like Mackay's
     whose tongue lolled now over his lower teeth
as he eyed the ball for the place-kick.
     His team mates were taller and more fair
     than Donnelan's broad-shouldered, brown-stubbled
brutes. Consider, for example, their
     saggy-buttocked lock as the scrum breaks.
     Consider the flapping breeze-blown folds of fat
on pumping stumpy legs as he retreats.
     Consider this; and then compare the pale
     blue-veined marble of our three-quarter's firm
muscled upper thigh, glimpsed when he
     feeds the ball back from a further maul.
     Note the stud-marks bloody there, for neither team
is entirely naked. Note the hooker's
     commitment to the game, how, breaking away,
     he cuts down space, runs, swerves and keeps possession.
Note his mastery of grubber, chip and punt.
     Rewind the tape. For this is more than just
     another of O'Driscoll's stories. Try to ignore
the penny-sized needle bruises in close-up.
     None of our men are users. Scorn our opponents'
     chilled pillocks. Celebrate flesh returned to its element
of earth, the insistent inscription of rain.

SLEEPWALKER'S ROMANCE

Shoes were at the heart of it. That much was clear.
Luxurious shoes of all-assuaging suppleness.
And he had left them there. Wherever there was.
With the picnic stuff in the precinct or the shopping bags
on the hilltop. And now he was here. And here
was also subject to change at a moment's notice.
The back of a Morris Minor or the restaurant at Fortnum's.
But wherever here was, they were. Welcome and comforting.
His children. His parents. This or that beloved?
But the only shoes on offer were a pair of beat-up trainers.
Not Reeboks exactly. Never mind the fur-lined slipper.
So he had to head off along the hostile corridors.
The playground was wet and it was becoming dark
earlier than expected. And there were questions to answer.
He realised that by now someone else could have the shoes.
And he might never know if it was power or it was love.
That he was running from. That he was searching out.

OUT

Lucille had the letter in her bag and *gratitude, rightsize,*
learner strategy, corkscrewed in her mind,
as she took the stairs in twos, took the leave owing her,
left quickly, taking the stairs again, in no particular order.
She took the tube to where she'd left the car,
slunk in and, glancing up and left,
moved into traffic. She ventured vaguely northward.
Kilburn State, the Welsh Harp reservoir, slipped past to one side.
When Jazz FM faded, she scrambled, one hand in the shoe box,
for a tape. Not Gorecki. Not Neil Young Unplugged.
She fished for the cassette Khaleb had taped in Cairo.
Umm Khaltoun's plaintive singing. Rhythm and voice
passionate, unyielding, unintelligible to her
as she blocked out Hertfordshire. She found herself
in Hitchin, paid and displayed, considered her position, found
nothing useful to her but a poached egg and tea.
And yet continued, eastwards now, garden-ribbon pseudo-cities
opening to tall skies of the broad East Anglian plain
somewhere near Wallington, where Eric Blair was wed
and saw, near Manor Farm, a cart horse bullied by a boy.
She skirted Cambridge heading North, suppressing a regret,
attaining speed on dual-carriage A-roads,
dodging horse-boxes, seeing airfields to her right, slowing
to fields in harvest and Swaffham's Georgian square,
still unsatisfied, still not knowing what she sought.

Near Walsingham an older world erupted:
Gothic arches bare as neolithic bones, prayer-filled,
sanctimonious sanctuaries. She shivered, heading for the coast.
Between Wells-next-the-Sea and Sheringham, she bought
a ticket for the motor boat that takes you out
into the brown waters south of Blakeney Point,
where oyster catchers dive for food
and the diamond-glittering, brown-and-grey-skinned seals,
swivel and swim between sand bank and Arctic sound,
nurturing their young, adapting like the coastline to the tide.

EDIT

You could start rumours about rivals and substantiate them.
Invert the corporate planner's wall-chart. Secrete his fresh
pack of Post-Its in the marketing manager's drawer.
Then wait for the many-headed snake to do its surreptitious worst,
insinuating between desk and VDU, sliding behind vertical files,
past the *monstera* no-one bothered to water.
Prepare to profit, to be amused, to forget the whole thing.

At the end of lunch, instead of getting up from the table, and sneaking
half-reluctantly like the others back to your parking place,
linger with that magnificent she or he who switched the earth's
magnetic poles back then. Stay all afternoon, with a print
of the harbour at Mykonos, some fruit and drying bread.
Stay after the serious drinking, the singing, the talk of running away.
Stay as the foolish drinking starts.

But it would be wrong!
Some repeated phrase or loop you didn't recognise straight off.
As you sand your palms with stubble, facing the washroom mirror,
it becomes monstrously clear that this is Nixon's voice.
The background's different silence
tells you the phrase was recorded later,
spliced into the tape to disguise guilt.

40TH BIRTHDAY WITH CASSETTE DECK AND QUESTIONS

In the next room children come and go,
talking of Michelangelo
and other awesome dudes.
O'Driscoll is on his knees again,
deciding which cut of 'One Too Many Mornings'
to dub for the party tapes.

Is that a smell of burning?

He settles for an upbeat country treatment
from the Isle of Wight bootleg.
The blue-jeaned tolerant original
they'd be embarrassed by. And he's not ready yet
for the leather-coated stand-off of *Hard Rain*.

Should he risk a white suit?

Beginning a slow bowler's windmill
to ease his stiff shoulder,
he remembers a song of Pete Townshend's.
The line *I was just 34 years old*.

Will anybody come?

DIRECTIVE

from a line by Peter Porter

There will be no dogs.
Muscle relaxant techniques developed in the clean cities campaign
to go national. Private sponsorship will match
innovation capital in sheep-herding areas.

The public role of Corgis to be phased out.
Also increased competition for heritage manufacturers.
Alternatives to Elgar to be encouraged.
The new anthem: *A Nation now and then*.

The new religion: spiritualism.
Replace that back-street, ouija-tapping fraud
with a customer-focused chain. Agree quality thresholds
for contact with the dead, service length and ectoplasm.

And horticulture rationalised.
The unlovely rose uprooted, its antisocial thorns burnt on hilltop beacons,
seeds pulverised, different-shaded petals shredded,
making the land free for order and light.

Y HABRA TRABÀJO PARA TODOS

Canary, scarlet, oatmeal, azure, green.
I like the green best I think – the colour
of a young leaf or just ripe capsicum –
used here for half a face, or the profile
of a face, all but the pouch under one eye
that masquerades as a full-bellied dove.

A woman's bare arm – impossibly long –
unfolding sheaves of wheat, posters, what might be
rolls of cloth; more faces split by stalks; a clenched
fist clutching a flashlight or pick-handle,
holding up, in the patchy blue,
the bright lonely star of his country's flag.

Among the waxy cookery smears and jagged
blu-tack scars on our uneven kitchen wall,
the caption's bold lettering survives
with this ambiguous promise; for sixteen years
it's earned its place – this message from Allende's
republic – AND THERE WILL BE WORK FOR ALL.

TENDERNESS

Is it six weeks since he started to scan
the green perimeters of towns like these,
skirt small-scale neighbourhoods for playing fields
whose mists give way to the thin metal legs
of institutional tables? Today he walks
along a gaping line of opened hatches –
Volvo Estates or sun-roofed Sierras –
noting cardboard-housed crockery, batches
of film magazines, one ironing board
burn-stained, little-worn suits and dresses.
He's looking, if asked, for electrical goods
but has in mind a certain twin-tone box,
coated in thin plastic, latched like luggage,
he'll recognise even from this distance.

The cream loudspeaker grille might be badly
yellowed, or chipped near one of its curved
corners, but he'll pull out a sheaf of notes.
He'll take the Dansette home and then search out
(among loft debris, dusty mementoes
of his children's childhood) the paper bags
that store – some scratched and most in mismatched
sleeves – his old black vinyl discs.

                                      Sifting
Parlophone pound signs, ears labelled
eff eff double r, he'll select eight singles
to stack on the still shiny central spindle
and shift the arm across.

Then he'll notice
he's chosen Soul records mostly: dance
numbers where the word *man* repeats itself
or gets stretched across three bars by Percy Sledge.
None of them stick or jump and the last brings
Otis Redding's voice, soaring pure against
the tinny unimpressive backing sound,
imploring him to *try a little*. And that word.

YES IT IS

It was something to do with the two of us
learning to drive so late; and that collection
of misplaced singles, B-sides, e.p. tracks

and oddities like 'Komm, Gib Mir Deine Hand'
came with us on our first car trip across country.
The A40. Dennis Potter's road. From Metroland

past Oxford, stopping at Birdlip to glimpse blue
remembered hills, picnicking in the Forest of Dean,
then down through valley-heads to my parents' home.

There were moments of terror: an articulated
lorry pulling into our lane just as we passed
its tail-gate; and anxieties about direction,

and moments of dreadful fatigue. The boys
counted legs of pub signs. And the tape helped:
the early songs most. Ringo's 'Matchbox'

holding his nose, *jealous* rhyming with *as well as*
over a repeated rhythmic chord, and then
that song nobody quite recalled, as if it had been

lying in wait for our early middle age.
Three-part harmony. John and George
obliterating Paul, Liverpool masking Detroit.

Red and *blue* and the unspoken *black,*
as Lennon's voice splintered in the bridge,
mourning his mother as you mourned yours.

THE BORDER

The queue might take an hour we're told.
Meanwhile, there's this form to fill, a relic of the recent past.
Currency, traveller's cheques, purpose of visit.
On the seat behind, you doze at last,
your glasses slipping down your nose,
the adventure discarded on your lap,
crumpled between your elbow and the seat.

It's your birthday and we're crossing to a new landscape.
This morning we saw harvests piled on rolling plains,
the chimneys of collective bakeries,
sheds where cattle live out secret lives indoors.
Now the afternoon unfolds on strips of field
where horses pull a plough
and hay's stooked in tidy decorated sheaves.

They put up the signs to Helsinki
the year that you were born. We watched
hesitant steps break into a confident
uneven run, the beginnings of self-control.
New choices will be made, unmaking the past,
and you, half-grown, rub your eyes awake
to a new country, another year in which to live.

REVENANTS

It's this same train-rattled flat
that we find shelter in, after
a Bohemian summer storm, presaged by
dust-devils, cloud cover
and sudden corridors of wind.

The fretted rail of vine leaves
that framed our balcony has gone.
The cane chairs we left behind, seatless,
sprout long tendrils; they've lost
whatever strawberry or pistachio tint

made our neighbours covet them.
Against cracked plaster and bared stone,
a pear-tree has wound round the towering beech
in next door's abandoned garden.
Six metres up, it offers hard and tasteless fruit.

The broken-backed damp books
are Pavel's, who kept the place
through the barely breaking winter of our
London years. I take down
Hrabal's *I Served the King of England* and recall

a Saturday in Kew, the
year that he could visit us;
how Pavel pulled his loping form up the
wrought-iron spiral stair
to view the largest indoor plant in Europe,

touching the roof of the temperate house.
His vaulted cheekbones, his eyes
clear, blue, transparent as the sky through glass,
shaded by the foppish brim
of his unseasonal panama. Return won't bring

the great release we dreamed of
any more than exile did.
Faces altered by disease, age, or merely compromise
greet us back in Prague.
But summer storms end quickly here.

And, as in London, we seek
refuge in iron fantasies
of the Belle Époque: Petrín Hill's pastiche
of the Eiffel toweř,
or the hall of mirrors where versions of our selves,

mis-shaped, repeat themselves
in mocking parallels.
The bright blue eyes of the soldier across from us
on yesterday's train
shone under the blue of his United Nations cap,

as Pavel's did at Kew.
Fates that ensnare enchant us first.
The sketchbook on your knee awaits defining lines.
Light and shade to draw the moment
from its labyrinth, to still a resisting heart.

WORKING FROM HOME

Watching, through the open
French doors and conservatory glass, these birds queuing
    at the feeder, pecking
and spitting out nuts and seeds, submissively anointing
    their forefeathers
in the drinking bowl, I tidy a table, content with
    what's brought us here:
times of waiting or worry, or losing our patience,
    and days like these
when someone takes the children out and someone stays
    with papers to read.
One day you're at the wave-pool. Spread out on the floor
    are coursework folders:
teenage fiction, research on street-gangs, someone's response
    to Wesker's *Roots*
and Hamid's painful, broken story of escaping from Tehran.
    Shootings, disappearances,
a Pepsi Cola lorry overturned, unclean, its sticky bubbly fluid
    running in the streets.
Another day you're working. In the Science Museum
    Sam, Benedict and I
start the combine harvester, make counterweights for bridges
    or launch a rocket.
Inside one case an Edsel; further on the crooked foot-digger
    Hebridean crofters
called a caschcrom. By raising or lowering a handle,
    those too poor to plough
determined the depth of the groove they needed to cut
    in the sparse soil,
then gripped the wooden shaft and kick-started the share.

I was writing some review
that Saturday you and the children went to London Zoo.
                    Waiting in line
for llama rides, you thought you recognised the smiling, neat
                    and prematurely balding man
holding his son's hand just ahead, steadying him in the cart.
                    It turned out not to be,
you realised on the train coming home, another parent
                    from the local school,
but the man who'd won the Booker Prize for *Midnight's Children*.
                    Now you're upstairs
writing a reference for a nurse in your Literature class,
                    while I chop onions
and listen for our not quite warring sons. Though
                    the author of *Shame*
might fear to be seen with a child in public and the enclosing,
                    impoverishing mind
shouts 'Kill the Ba'hais' or plans forced migrations, at evening
                    perennial birdsong
brightens our garden. It doesn't make everything right, but
                    makes it easier,
the children bathed and read to, easier to touch another's hand,
                    or speak quietly,
so when night does come what we notice is an arc of moonlight
                    curved by the ribbed
plastic roof above us – no rainbow or triumphal arch, but
                    what work tends toward –
efforts of love: attention, desire, holding darkness at bay.

PART THREE
1998-2016

For now abideth —
Politics, Art and Love, these three, and of these the greatest
Is — but I am not the Shepherd Idean to settle the question —
Politics, Art, and Love, and the greatest of these is the purest.

—Arthur Hugh Clough,
'Amours de Voyage' (Manuscript A)

FEBRUARY

We walked back and forth from the library,
preparing for some high leap: sunlight catching
the tallest spume of the shopping centre fountain.

Something we owe to the past made our elders
stand, kneel and then sit in buildings
warmed by a hope for something better.

That monogrammed leather trunk
we use to keep the dresses
you can't throw away came ahead of you.

Just so the twisted black
of the ornamental cherry's bark
breaks out in gluey scars

that papery pink peeps through,
ballooning to the rumoured candy cloud
the street stands still for sight of.

Imported, fitted to this soil
but fruitless, its grace
sustains what reason
could not argue for: its place.

AFTERWARDS

The ritual of open-evening wall-displays.
In the maths corridor, she came on neatly-shaded graphs,
histograms, colour-coded pies. *Our Leisure Time.*
TV, homework, shopping, sports and games
jostling with visits to friends and paper rounds.

On Raymond's bar chart, a single column towered above
its neighbours' dwarfish blocks, its simple label *Out.*
It didn't take her long to bring to life from that
an image of the gangly, crop-haired boy, dangling
on a swing too small for him, in the wet and leafstrewn park.

And it seems no time has passed when, in an unfamiliar pub,
a voice calls out, *Remember me, Miss!*
He tells her how he went back to show them all:
his uniform, the noise his boots made on the tiling floors.
Mr Jones said, let us know before, another time.

He expected Ireland, got the Gulf. *There's lots of stuff*
you never hear about. This big ditch we dug… Afterwards
he got out quick. Health reasons. But the training gets you work.
Security. Firearms' research. *But I was always clumsy, Miss.*
He gestures with his splintered lower arm.

ECHOES

They called it the second summer of love
but they dressed as if for the first.
Clive's sawdust-red hair hung lank
and long as Zal Yanovsky's and
Indira peered at the Browning essay
that poked out of her copy of *Vogue*
through Janis Joplin's specs.

Even their teacher, pushing forty,
could risk a narrow paisley-patterned tie.
A late September sun blessed
the afternoon and their lesson took that light.
Passion outraced wit as the first act closed;
the hall and imagined hills rang
to Olivia's, Viola's reverberate love.

One had the wild hair and quizzing eyes of
Tim Buckley on the cover of *happy sad*.
He had too much to say at first,
started coming late, missed lessons,
disappeared for weeks, returned
and half explained. Promises were made.
He vanished once again.

He sent a postcard from New York:
dog-sitting in a loft. Then home
and hospital. Was it the drugs they said
he sold that fired his brain?
The gossiping air knew best. He came
for a reference with his Macedonian girlfriend;
each of them a gentle refugee.

THE SECRET MINISTRY

Šumplica Novakova laughed
as she zigzagged from queue to queue
in the cabbage market,
her last purchase always
the braided poppy-seed rolls.
Her bright silk blouses –
lilac, crimson or whichever colour
her hidden calendar required –
lightened the day,
when she broke and shared the eucharist
among carefully invited friends.

When a mate from the plant
made a fool of himself with a girl,
I'd invite him home for a meal.
He'd meet Jinka and the kids.
We'd drink a few beers, eat dumplings
and meat seasoned with a herb
that might recall his wife's name.
I gave absolution under my breath,
making a sign in the palm of my hand.

Now they've given the postal workers'
museum back to the Cistercians.
I've a collar to wear and memos
from Rome about Mexican practices.
The lads are friendly enough,
but look at me
like a guy with something to sell,
some multinational's rep.

Last week, I saw Šumplica
in the marketplace,
finding the best fruit
as ever. Once, she whispered
what would not be silenced.
Now, she spoke out loud,
steadying her bicycle. It was
after all love we ministered to
so no regrets. She laughed
as the pigeons scattered,
flying off God knows where.

THE TAMBOURICA PLAYER'S WIFE

His stained fingers scratched
at the sympathetic strings.
Next to him the Romany
girl was singing the usual
tales of love's abandon and
abandoned love. Songs
of freedom: with wild eyes
like the skinny cats in the
locked Serbian church.

What lines his face,
I paid for too. So when
her voice twins with his
lamenting the times, it's
my heart floods. If not for
the nation saved, for the
future he stole, the island
cottage we should have had,
the smell of cypress after rain.

SUNDAY MORNING

Stevens, MacNeice and The Velvet Underground.
A lightness rising to a cloudless sky.
Too tired for sleep or love we drive together
out of numbness to a different town.
The long ponds where we used to feed the ducks,
the stretch of green that climbs to the cathedral,
the breakfast, the bookshop we trust will
take gravity from us, floating away.

But now the radio plays Haydn, a piece
in F sharp minor, contrived we're told
to solve a problem in the Esterhazy Court,
so in the last movement the players left
singly, snuffing out their candles, leaving
the last couple to hold the stage alone.

CELLULAR

We'd grit our teeth in trains as the brash
human resources manager turned the seat
next to us into her office, or blush
as privacies invaded
our poorly air-conditioned space.

But we had also seen a strong jaw soften,
a head tilting towards its own shoulder,
murmuring to the small world
it cradles and creates. And smiled
as the straight-faced colleague
danced in the car park,
her head back, laughing
like someone living on another plane.

And later would hear how,
in Manhattan, a husband tapped again
the digits he had tried to reach all day
beneath rubble, atoms, ashes, dust
until the voice mail's memory could take
no more spoken words or text.

DIGITAL

Like a girl with a new pony,
she's happy enough to pose
for the lens. The fun's on pause

but it's something for the folks
at home; a souvenir of the tour
to speed ahead of her on-line.

It's asked of her; she looks
almost bored in her boyish
t-shirt and camouflage pants,

which is so like a uniform,
it takes a while to see
the casual clothes are army

issue. This is a dog-lead
not a bridle. This is no
pony, just a naked man.

THE LENGTH OF SPRING

Peace is possible. The Amnesty dove's
still stickered to the window of the house
we didn't buy from you. And now you're housed
in a wicker coffin, a hamper of
the good things you were and will be, in the love
of your still friends, in the Friends' meetinghouse.
We stay to watch your children shoulder the spades
they dug into the moist earth to cover you;
and talk as if words could recover you
to the cold air, to the light's sharpest blades.

The same fierce brightness picks out the parade
against the war, and we remember you
at the month's end as we move shoe and shoe
ahead along the Embankment, early
arrivals buying new badges, nearly
losing one another by Westminster tube
and dawdling down Whitehall, enjoying the true
absurdity of *Make Tea Not War*. Dearly
the young in black entwine themselves for warm,
lest love fail, should nothing stop the war.

Another world is possible. As the war
draws near, a slogan on a lapel draws
smiles and nods, but subdued by will and force
we stumble in. I block out the war,
listening to Jacobi's *Iliad* not the news,
until the statues start to fall across
the screens and grudging praise of 'moderate loss'
is heard beyond the dusty haze
of crazed cuneiform tablets, wrecked houses
and orphaned children's distanced cries.

IN THE PALM OF MY HAND

Starting from the new towers' atria and in-house concessions,
        you find a way to where this yellow stone stands,
slant and widdershins, not far from the lovely naked bones of
        Catherine and William Blake. The scant
non-conformist burying ground of Bunhill Fields (hardly fields,
        neat and weeded pathways lead to the chart
that marks the graves of the remembered names) – cuts between
        trunkways hurrying noisily north of Moorgate.
Not being the man in the brown ankle-length coat who leaves a
        single flower in water here, move on to Spitalfields
past tumbled histories of housing, a church turned concert hall,
        estates and enterprises, posters stuck to walls.

Put your finger on the map and start from there, from any there,
        to see through the side window of Westminster
Public Libraries (Marylebone Branch) this intent face diving
        for the meaning his gloved finger points halfway
down the page towards. In puffa jackets, woollen hats or baseball
        caps, carrying their goods in supermarket shopping
bags, faces of all nations, hurry, saunter, cross your path, face
        or follow you. The new bagel bar. The chemists
established 1814. Blue plaques for poets in Poland Street
        and Polish *Newsweek* in the cornershops. A lowslung
bus snakes and humps round a formal square. Cream walls
        steeped in a sudden honey of late afternoon light.

And a river moves through it, walled but washing against
       the window of a Limehouse pub, alive to the warming
of the world's waters, the exchanges of currents and currency.
       Light flashes intermittently from the pyramid top
of Canary Wharf, and the yellow-brown water itself is pulled
       into little peaks of reflected light. We saw it from Waterloo
Bridge on that march from Lincoln's Inn to the Imperial War Museum;
       then sat on the green lawn near those great guns
as Tony Benn shared memories of a century's dissent.
       And upriver – wisteria on white walls, gated communities,
joggers and rowers glide past a jazz club, a cricket pitch
       the entrance to a canal, public gardens, palaces.

And something like this was in his mind when he turned from
       that enormous blast, looking for those in his care
that he'd ferried through Islington and Finsbury, and saw
       twisted metal upstairs on what now looked like
a tourist bus. So that when help arrived and what could be
       made good began to be done, what was there but
to follow those walking away, westward past the dome that
       keeps Jeremy Bentham's mummified remains,
past busy hospitals beneath the telecom tower or Arab cafés
       along the Harrow Road, until somewhere near
Wormword Scrubs a stranger saw the blood on his jacket
       and helped him to the Casualty in Du Cane Road.

If we open the door, if we open our eyes, everything here
        seems paved or clothed, labelled or priced, stamped
with its destination, encrypted with its time of arrival.
        It is the sidelong looks more in recognition than
desire that release the unchanelled: the palest hint of
        a blush, sky in the mirrorglass of offices, what
a girl called 'that Thomas Hardy kind of foolishness'.
        The bite of the pickled chilli in the pitta salad
in Gig's fish bar in Tottenham Street has it. The heron
        standing on the effluent pipe looks out for it.
Daily we brush against it or glimpse it beyond our touch.
        What we walk through, fail to say, or try to hold.

DELIVERY

(i.m. M. Donaghy)

Five minutes into your memorial
service, my knee is jiggling to
a reel you wrote at twenty-five,

half your life away. My memory
and ear struggle to end the line
Donne wrote for such as you. You'd

find the word, as easy as breathing out:
rest of their bones and soul's (   )
four syllables; something to rhyme with free.

SONG

I passed the warning signs.
My skin was scratched with briars.
I found the hidden lake
where the heron's wing caught fire.

My skin was scratched with briars.
My cuffs were grey and torn.
Where the heron's wing caught fire
I felt as if transformed.

The surface glittered red and green
beyond the boundary wire
as if a sparkling stone
nestled in my palm.

Beyond the boundary wire,
I found the hidden lake
nestling, in my palm,
beyond the warning signs.

THAT YEAR

She is steadying
her arm along the brick
wall of the railway bridge,

paused after hurrying
sweet swift uncounted drinks
with no reason, and sings

that without her looking
autumn has gone running
on its paths of orange;

only a vast moon
is left in the low
half-lit sky. An apple,

she says, sliced by
the slim-bladed trees.

THE FOLDING STAR

Horace, *Odes I ix*
Tacita Dean, *Michael Hamburger*

Let's not ask if this is the last time
we watch the sea off the Eastern coast
erode the land, wave by grasping wave.
Look instead through the pimpled panes
at the firm red glow of evening light
on brick. Lift your eyes and wait until
the deepening blue reveals a pinch
of light, a planet-shaped white promise.

While we talk, hours gather to take flight.
In a neglected space where children
wander, we've seen wild Eden-coloured
fruit projected on a wall, fruit a
poet grew from seed resisting the
damage of geography and time.

THE CAVALCANTINE LURE

Cavalcanti, *Sonnet XVIII*

A pretty face, the very heart of reason,
the expert's dry indifference to rank,
the song of birds and lovers' reasoning
and boats lit all along the southern bank.
Purest air; dawn's first whitest hour
and white snow falling where there is no wind,
backwaters and meadows gemmed with flowers
– gold and silver with sea-blue gems inlaid.

Match such, the poet says with your spare praise
of love, or the one who's loved, and his words
are red-hot coals that we can walk across;
like sunlit metal, the pealing bells heard
clearly in the twilight of years and days
with talk of songs and stings, of heart and loss.

SOUTHERLY

Yves Bonnefoy, *Á la Voix de Kathleen Ferrier*

Sweet knowingness, a crystal fog goodbye,
swordstrokes almost in silence, bladelight veiled.
He praises the grey tone in the voice that
wavers in the distant reaches of song.
Lost song. And beyond its pure form trembles
a further song. Light and the death of light –
and a note higher than passion or pain.
A real place in the unreal stream.

Her voice moves in its own space, and moves too
in his mind that drifts between banks, knowing
extremes. Somehow I've turned up next to him,
outside the closed museum, imagining
the apple tree burning with magic, the
miniature marbles cold in the vitrine.

FOR ERNEST SEIGLER

I came across your books last week
in the Ealing Oxfam,
Rilke's *Orpheus* in the New York
first edition of the German text

that will keep as a gift
for Christmas. A Robert Frost
I knew, but didn't know:
A Witness Tree. (I couldn't give

somehow, good money for
the Ronald Bottrall from
Tambimuttu's press. But
took the Sidney Keyes.)

There they were, with your name in ink
and '46 in subscript.
So in the dying days of this year,
sixty years after

you spent hard earned,
I'd guess, cash
at Better Books, 92-
94 Charing + Road,

I noticed the tiny
bookplate for the shop
and, turning a page,
the line drawing of Frost,

youngish for his fifties
and already outliving
the poet friend his
face here reminds me of.

The poem I read on to
speaks of a 'day
no shadow
crossed but ours'.

And today is set fair
to unravel as such
another movement
from clear clearly to clear:

the sun mirrored
by the river's small waves,
music like a muffled joy
playing in a back room.

Such easy heights or depths
give form to what is passing
some sense of compensation
for what it lacks in length.

SNOW DAYS

In a week where you wake at half three
three days in a row, and even the water
which ought to spiral down gaily
beneath your feet in the shower, won't
but rises greyly to your shins before
slipping shamefacedly away, it's alright
to hope for the morning call that says:
Forget about today. We don't need you

to come in. And the children head for the hill
with trays as toboggans. And the young have
coloured scarves and hats to stand out against
the white surprise of everything, while we
slide back beneath covers enjoying what is
known and warm and feels like righteous sin.

CRISIS MANAGEMENT

A wasp enters the room. The class flashes
alive in this sharp light of the instant.
Each takes a role in the pantomime
of gender: gasping and shrinking back with
a terrible screeching of chairs, or rolling
a textbook into the form of a club.
He's seen this before and shushes offers
to kill, shaking dregs from his mug.
He traps the frightened buzz against the glass,
slides a worksheet under the rim, lifts it
and sends the creature to a dazed freedom.
A window is closed, to mock applause.

But a bird in the exam hall. This is not
expected. When it skeeters and clatters
overhead, invigilators reach for poles
helpless as it lets drop its white
sticky bomb within inches of a desk.
In the still silent panic one begins
to hear whispers of evacuations,
and someone hurries to a phone.

AFTER HERRICK

I was delivering
with what talent,
verve or conviction
I could muster
some element
no doubt of the
heritage strand
of the National
Curriculum
(revised), when
a Julia or
Celia took from
her pencil case
a handful of
coloured markers
and started to
construct log fences
or oxers – delicate,
suspended by their
own weight – on
the desk in front
of her. Absorbed
by the task and
with half an ear
open no doubt
to Juliet's fate,
she inhabits a
bubble of youth
I would not burst,
that time's transhifting
has failed to wear away.

CERNUNOS

Some came in trucks, bedded down as ballast
between the manifold and the manifest,
or in white vans hidden behind white goods,
or clinging on carriage tops to Ebbsfleet.
Others came by sea. Imagine hazel
tarred and twined or wicker threaded into
basket-boats, the recruiting sergeant's shilling,
or furs brought downriver by raft. Then this.

Part of my mind has forgotten itself
already, slipped into the off-white wall
of the interrogation room, finding
faces etched in the floorstains, ready to
be investigated like a fragment
of text scraped onto pottery or bone.

GILGAMESH IN URUK

Forty klicks into enemy lines
a Humvee on recon
tilts into this city seeing
'dust and hajis mostly'.

Further back, a figure
looks beyond the wall
as bodies float downriver
nameless, unnumbered.

He had fought fire
and lost a friend
gigantic as myth.
And death was much
like birth, with its screams
and blood and tears.

SOUTHBANK

'After the waters rose
and the wave made
a wall that halved the sky,
the wind lifted
my house, shook it
like dice from a cup
and landed me here.
It pierces the plain
glass front of an eighth-floor
apartment, scattering
the minimalist shelving
jumbling the magazines,
and posters, driftwood
of city days, fragments
snatched from the crash.

So I come to the river
at the end of the day
for songs that echo
an elsewhere: the
mountains of Mourne,
the river where we sat
down to the hum of
disco from a cruiser,
dark Spanish guitars,
a distant Chinese flute.

PRAYER

Boethius *'O stelliferi conditor orbis'*

Star-maker, world conductor,
turbine of the rapid turning
sky, moon-pacifier that stills
the satellite to rest in sun —
letting it pale in the off weeks,
letting the beauty of the lesser
lights shine within its darkened horns —
force that in the evening's first
moments sends Venus chasing
the frigid stars across the
dark blue, violet and indigo
backdrop, until she rises
shamefaced, pale as Lucifer
in the morning-fresh sky;

thermostat of the globe,
force that, when the winter
finally lets leaves fall, limits
our view of their crisp curled
burial to the shortest hours and
in summer's violent heat,
when the body calls out for love,
quickens the passage of dark;
what the North Wind strips
from elm and oak and beech
the Gulf Stream soothes into bud;
what was sown in the days of
the Joy Star, the dog days will
see toasting in full crop;

if everything in nature points
to underpinning laws that
run inside the veins and reach
the distant stars, why have
all made and living things
been turned to whims of chance,
so that winds pull trees
from their roots, the sea rises
against us, the poles weep?
why has human desire
played with the balance
of things so that no-one
can judge the weight of
a coin in justice's hands?

why do the slides of fortune
shift things so that torturers
tread on the necks of men,
fraud smoothes its coiffeured
hair and what should shine
clear shivers in the dark
with only the pulse's rhythm
to measure our lives against?

TITYUS

In Michelangelo's drawing
this voluptuous male reclines,
one hand tied to a pillow of stone
while the other seems to slide below
the belly of the broad-spanned,
muscular, soft-feathered bird.
Daily it pecks his liver,
sensuality's last square.
Nightly his strength returns.

Stanley walks around the frame
to see the figure traced again.
On the verso it emerges
a resurrected Christ.

On a preserved railway platform,
a dozen years ago,
he saw a kiss between women:
a face upturned, something
half suppressed, half understood,
hanging like steam in air,
compressed like veins in rock.

THREE SISTERS

— for Pussy Riot

I did go to Moscow,
Yakaterina says,
to stand in the cathedral
and sing a jagged song
against the Patriarch, the fixer
the smooth word and the suit.

I did go to Moscow,
says Maria Alyokhina,
because we're trained
from childhood
to forget the child's
unwelcome question.

I did go to Moscow,
Nadezhda also says,
because work is not enough
to burst the corporate
gangsters' smugness;
we must speak as holy fools.

Unshielded protectors,
dance and stamp your feet;
stomp and shout your song
until your words drown out
the limousine-driven cross,
the cassock and the boot.

TIPPING POINT

As the grabbing claw
digs into General Waste,
dust rises to our level.

We taste it at the back
of the throat, in the nose,
fanning it from our eyes.

From the boots of cars,
methodically, we lift
worn, damaged

– or just outdated –
consumer goods.
Threadbare carpets,

inkjet printers,
cardboard casings,
hard plastic toys

chipped crockery,
broken tools, video-
cassettes, virus-

checking software.
We empty bags of
paper into the pit.

Out come tumbling:
style magazines,
political manifestos,

football programmes,
workshopped poems,
unsent letters of love.

And this is not a metaphor.
The grabbing claw grabs on.

HIS GRANDSON CONSIDERS THE PHILOSOPHY
OF MARTIN HEIDEGGER

Being here
is full of wonder, yes —
the tastes of banana or broccoli
the noise I make with my finger on my lips
and faces to look at, not mine.

Does the Sandman puppet
feel what I feel
when a you goes away?
I don't think so.

If I put a triangle block
in the triangle window,
or a round block in the round hatch
of the shape-sorting house,
that is correct.

But the doubled image of me
in the strengthened window glass
is not correct, but true.
I laugh at the truth.
I clap my hands.

JUTLAND

'Unhappy and at home' (Seamus Heaney)

i

How often had we wrapped
our mouths around that phrase
in classrooms: *Some day*
I will go to Åarhus.

And here, by Ryanair,
we were, snow still unthawed
at the side of the road,
crocuses and snowdrops

making a stand for life
against the flat green earth
and the solid wall of sky.
The exchange house opened

its doors to us, each in
the white centre of a wall
like openings on a stage
where we'd play another life.

Unlikely tourists among
the warm and brightly clad,
we were looking out for
the stained and peat-brown face

we'd talked about in class.
Out of town at Moesgård
we saw the Grauballe find –
throat slit, smooth, exceptionally

preserved. The museum
could have been the manor-
house hotel from *Festen,*
hiding who knows what hurts.

ii

Afterwards we walked down
to the little stony bay
for our first close look
at the still, cool Baltic.

As for the Tollund Man,
he wasn't to be found in
Åarhus; instead he was
kept near to his digging,

out there in Silkeborg.
We set out on the small
Arriva train, the day
it happened to be shut.

But they let us in, while
they prepared a children's
display of Yggdrasil
and we stood face-to-face

with the foetal body
and its broad sleeping
face that was the spirit
itself of gentleness.

We walked quietly back
past the bobbing pleasure
boats tied up alongside
the out-of-season lake.

iii

The girl on the platform
is setting out from here
with rucksack, wheelie-case
and black portfolio.

The rhythms of their speech
and the familiar sounds
that shape their words persuade
us that we understand

what passes between her
and the others – maybe
neighbours or her mother's
friends. *London*, they say, with

a beam of happiness
for her. This must be where
she is heading, moving
out of the Midlands

town with its small comforts
to a widening world.
They smile as if telling her
she need not be afraid.

A TRUE STORY

Up! High! The child laughs pointing through the window
        at the two birds in the guttering that runs under
        the grey slate roof.

The white bird with its mobile head monitoring the street;
        the young grey-feathered bird scuttering end-to-end.

'The situation is beyond control', Councillor Brown (Locals
        First) addresses the meeting. He need not remind them
        of the incident at the harbour.

'We want our town back', he is sputtering, scanning the hall.
        'The time has come for a cull!'

The white herring gull is dragging a knotted white plastic bag
        from the fly-tipped pile behind the disused phone-box
        pulling and scratching as it goes.

It takes four gulls screeching and tugging to tear it apart
        and feast on the leftover Chinese takeaway.

Miss Dawson (Liberal Elect) reminds the meeting of the
        recent oil spillage. The effort and expense
        undertaken in the aftermath.

Cleaning feathers with a toothbrush and detergent.
        'Surely this showed us at our best?'

GPS tracking of birds in the town reveals a nesting
        site in the cinema currently showing
        Finding Dory.

The gull population, which is native not migratory,
        consists of 239 breeding pairs.

Doctor Triomphe (Third Way) offers the assembly
        his preferred solution: a transparent ceiling.
        A dome of rare device,

using recycling technology, guano a key constituent.
        The gulls would pay for the roof!

Ha-ha-ha!   *Meeeeww!*   *Ha-ha-ha! Ha-ha-ha!*
    Keow!   *Keow!*
    Huoh-huoh-huoh.

Klee-ew?   *Klee-ew?*   *Ha-ha-ha! Ha-ha-ha!*
    Meeeeww!   *Huoh-huoh-huoh.*

LOOSE LEAF

These old green or orange
paperbacks are falling
apart on us. Pages
dropping out, tobacco-
coloured, flaking at the
edges. Incipient
autumn is outside us
too: the bright yellow slips
of willow, or still green
oak-leaves curling as if
left too near the fire.
The low afternoon sun
warm on the back of the neck
throws light on the spire across
from us and on the white
rose among the tight black
curls of the schoolgirl
checking her smartphone.
In the park we can admire
flashes of yellow and
red on the beak of this
coot-like bird and marvel
at the gloriousness
of now, unbothered
by the evening's chill.

ACKNOWLEDGEMENTS

Some of these poems appeared previously in the following publications in print and online: *Acumen, Ambit, Agenda, And other poems, Aquarius, Brittle Star, Cracked Lookingglass, Dog, Green Lines, Green River Review* (USA), *Morning Star, New Boots and Pantisocracies, New Statesman, New Walk, North, nthposition, Numbers, The Observer, Oxford Magazine, Poetry Durham, Poetry London, Poetry Oxford, Poetry Review, The Rialto, Shearsman, Sheffield Thursday, The SHOp, Siting Fires, Smiths Knoll, Southern Review* (USA), *Tears in the Fence, Times Educational Supplement, Times Literary Supplement, Verse, York Literary Review.*

Some poems were also included in the following anthologies: *Singing Brink* (Arvon, 1988), *The Spaces of Hope* (Anvil, 1998), *The Heart in Autumn*, (Periscope, 2001), *The Captain's Tower* (Seren, 2011), *Catechism: Poems for Pussy Riot* (English PEN, 2012), *Newspaper Taxis* (Seren, 2013), *The Arts of Peace: A Centenary Anthology* (Two Rivers Press, 2014), *The Best of Poetry London* (Carcanet, 2014) and *The Poet's Quest For God* (Eyewear, 2016).

'Cernunos' was commissioned by Bank Street Arts, Sheffield for the exhibition *In Their Own Words* (2008). 'Brief Encounter' won fourth prize in the City of Cardiff International Poetry Competition, 1992. 'Pornography' won first prize in the 1995 Sheffield Thursday poetry competition. 'Tenderness' was a winner in the Blue Nose Poets-of-the-Year competition 2001.

Some poems appeared in the pamphlets *The Secret Ministry* (2001) and *Tenderness* (2004) published by Smith/Doorstep, or in the collections *The Interrupted Dream* (Anvil, 1985), *Keeping Time* (Salt, 2008) and *Imagined Rooms* (Salt, 2010).

Grateful thanks are due to Todd Swift, Edwin Smet and the Eyewear team for the care shown and advice given in the preparation of this volume.